Things I should have said, but never did

Jennifer Dellow

ISBN-13: 978-1544090498
ISBN-10:1544090498

iii

David, the first friend I ever had. Like streetlights scattered along a path; you can't make the distance shorter but you certainly light the way home.

CONTENTS

ACKNOWLEDGMENTS

This is possible because of everyone I have met. Their experiences have become my memories.

S

The scar around my neck;
Like a red velvet trim,
Entices and lures all
The souls that I've met.

The calm, still road;
Belies all the chaos,
That occurred that Winter
When he couldn't be tamed.

The hot and cold waves;
Like bathing in nausea
Wash over my conscious
And I'm left here alone.

M

Under a tree,
A man sits to rest.
He is in no hurry
But each day is a test

He wants to be alone
But he misses someone
He wants to be happy
But has no patience for fun

He cannot live in the moment
He cries when he's hurt
He's a creature of habit
He must wear the same shirt

He thinks he's not worthy,
Nobody is sad with his goodbyes.
He doesn't know what it feels like
To look into his eyes

It's not about appearance-
He never tries to be kind.
A soul that is blackened,
Like his heart and his mind

DF

Lips can be stopped
And tongues can be caught
But my eyes always betray
My hearts true thought

I may deny words to your face
Only my pride knows it's true
Because the pain from rejection
Doesn't compare to pain from you

The heart forever serious
The brain foretells a joke
All I need is a little push
And the words are spoke –

Ich werde dich immer lieben
An all die Dinge, die wahr ist
Die welt ist immer leer
Falls sie nicht uber Sie

K

The wind has brought a different air
Across the skies, across my face.
My lungs expand as much as they dare,
I feel the change and increase the pace.

I'd never felt the fear of love,
Until I awoke that rainy night.
I realised then the time was wrong,
He'd wound the string around my kite.

It's hard to glance towards his window,
Not knowing for certain if he exists.
The lights do change-proving nothing
I long to know but cannot persist.

AD

When I can only see the starlight
When the world won't let me be
I reach for you – my precious soul guide
You bring the sun that lets me see

When I can only hear me calling
When the only route is down
I reach for you my rising companion
You sit me high – put on my crown

When I can only feel the darkness
When I'm tied against the mast
I'll reach for you; my only comfort
Who accepts my present, future and past

HM

How can it be so quiet?
When you were such a big life.
I remember seeing your face
As you dozed next to your wife.

You never spoke about it,
I suppose you kept it in a box.
Along with friends and family-
There was just too many locks.

Oh why leave so soon?
I longed for so much more-
A man now forever silent,
A fragile soul changed by war.

S

Being here in this cream haze
The weeks have merged – no more days
The bopping of the record plays

Across the bank of chestnut blue
A seesaw watches all I do
Here or not, I'll think of you

Cryptic bottles are thrown my way
Half are real – others just what I'll say
It wants control but I won't lay

J

Everyday feels exactly the same
I must start again and play the game
Cannot think clearly – the scar has maimed

I'm loneliest when I'm in a crowd
Can't stand noise – everything's too loud
I've done some things and I'm not proud

I mustn't rely on there being a moon
Can feel it coming, coming and soon
I'm out of sync – it's always noon

So lie back and take my potion
And calm the words; the brains commotion
It's come and gone; - swept like the ocean

SF

He lived and sighed
Just like a ghost
A soul meant for higher things
It floats and moves
Around this Earth
Hoping that the sunrise brings

He listens and he thinks
The whirring brain
Even sleep doesn't give a rest
The mind is quick
But he moves slowly
In this world just as a guest

His face is masked
To all but something
Can a spirit unlock his heart?
He sends his soul
Out every night now
The cord could snap if we should part

R

I want to leave this life with you
I don't care where we go
The world can smile or turn its back
At our footprints in the snow

The world is ours or so it seems
We both live lives out of sight
The mind over rules and steals the days
But at least we can get back the night

We will always stand apart on our plinths
Through every one of occurring skies
Our words will be bible – face resembling the sun
I just want to look into your eyes

PJ

I've been cast adrift
The ropes been cut
I'm trying to live
I want things but…

The heart's not with me
A pain too raw
I'm trying to live
But then I saw…

My body's caged with
A mind free as a bird
I'm trying to live
And then I heard…

Sighs never echo

Sighs never echo
I have been told
They rebound only sadness
The longing that's cold

If I could hear them
I would surely be deaf
I just want silent kisses
To fill my last breath

Awaken to a new morning

Awaken to a new morning
The sun through the window,
Envelopes the fear-
That ails the night.

The leaves bow to Autumn,
They know what they've seen,
Steadfast and calm-
They're guardians of light.

The day starts grey,
And ends in black.
My eyes like the windows-
Splattered with rain.

Talking to you again;
How can this be?
Your words are the plasters,
Over my scars.

The glue has now gone,
Lost in the rain-
From the face of the shamed
That did no wrong

Why would you help?
When it costs you nothing,
To pull a soul away-
From their untimely death.

A lock that has rusted,
Is loved all the same;
I wouldn't change the time-
That weathered the air.

DD

Can my heart be filled no more
Than the happiness that I feel?
Walking along the bourgeois Straße
I hold his hand to make it real.

Back at home he creates my comfort,
As I experience this ebb and flow.
Every moment is a golden envelope
The strongest man I'll ever know

Fading Faces

Fading faces,
From those hiding places;
The labyrinth corridor
With too high beams

Mumbled voices,
A handbook of choices;
The rusted sidecar
Asleep only in my dreams.

Cursory glances,
Towards forgotten chances;
The solitary sunset
Unraveled at the seams.

OW

His strong deep voice and towering statue – His eyes seem to take possession

I can't help my thoughts, I'm under control – His life has become an obsession

I appreciate the art, his form; his life – with each day I feel a step nearer

Life contradicts my heart, my soul, my essence – I'm sure I was born in the wrong era

What is my name? I can no longer tell – I feel warm and where I belong

I wish I was there, or thought of at least – as the subject of Rochester's Song

S

I knew you were going to hurt me,
I saw the look that was in your eye;
As you throttled out my sanity-
With violent words which made me cry.

People ran down towards the Harbour,
Shouting "Please, oh do take note!"
But you held my hand and was smiling,
As, I stepped aboard your boat.

Days of stormy clouds and thunder,
It's been weeks since I saw the pier.
Cast adrift now with a monster;-
Who plays up to all my fear.

Will I ever see a lighthouse?
All passers-by just stand and wave.
I may be calm, and fine and smiling;-
But deep down I need to be saved.

Upon the Stage

Upon the stage
Where I belong
I am not heard
Although I sing my song

The world is silent
Or am I too loud?
I am alone in my head
And in amongst the crowd

Touching the Moon

Black and white; grey and green
It was the first night we had been seen
A supportive arm right from the start
I didn't want us to be apart

A waving hand greeted my eyes
My heart leapt – that's no surprise
Escorted to the coloured door
We walked across a fearful floor

There may have been music; I didn't hear
There were others; but their faces aren't clear
Throughout that night I only saw blue
My hood was down and I felt brand new

Newly dyed eyes or different view?
I wanted you to see all that I knew
A smile and words which made me think
Standing so far, yet here on the brink

Standing then sitting, our souls were too close
Hearing a rhythm of what our ribs enclose
The thing between us is only air
I want to say…..but do I dare?

We took a ride to trepidation gate
In no hurry; didn't want to be-late
Swept up and wrapped; within a cocoon
I felt an experience – like touching the moon

DC

I'm asking you to stay;
The words are finally here.
A sun that never sets -
A mind that's rarely clear.

If it snows than we could see;
Solid proof that we exist.
Knocking on the door of fate -
Only the strongest will persist.

I'm asking you to see;
It isn't hard to find.
We are deaf to loudest words -
Here in front; but we are blind.

ABOUT THE AUTHOR

Jennifer Dellow is a 32-year-old life aficionado with a desire to allow all parts of her personality to have the floor. She has had a passion for poetry and prose since her childhood that has continued vehemently into her adulthood.

Jennifer lives in England and when she's not writing, she enjoys obsessing over David Bowie and Orson Welles. You can follow her on Twitter or visit her blog **https://ninjanerdflewlone.wordpress.com** for more delirious insights into her world.

Twitter: **@JenJenJen1385**

Facebook: **A Menagerie of Letters**